MASTERING EVERYDAY ENGLISH CONVERSATIONS

A PRACTICAL GUIDE

CHESHTA TUTEJA

Contents

I

Chapter 1: How to Introduce Yourself

The first impression is the last impression. This fits in each and every aspect starting from our appearance to our communication skills. The way a person introduces himself gives an idea of his conversation abilities. There is no doubt that confidence plays a significant role in communicating, but having the right knowledge about how to do it adds the cherry to the cake.

Ways to Introduce Oneself:

1. Hello, I am Anita.
2. Hi, my name is Anita.
3. Or you can even just say your name: "Hey, Anita," accompanying it with a hand shake (if in person) (preferred for informal introduction).

Common Mistakes We Make While Introducing Ourselves

A. Never use ***"Myself"*** for introducing yourself, as it is a Pronoun, and a Pronoun cannot be used for introduction.
B. Avoid using ***"This is."*** It is used commonly to introduce a third person. So, while introducing yourself, avoid using "This is."
C. Always use a greeting before introducing yourself.

Things That Can Be Added in Your Introduction:

1. Your **Interests**
2. **Adjectives** to define yourself as a person
3. **Place** where you belong
4. **Achievements**, if any
5. What you **Aspire** to be

Note: These should be included only when asked in an informal conversation and mandatorily in a formal conversation.

Let's see some examples of how one can introduce herself/himself in a decent yet impactful way.

They are Vikas and Prateek, who are always low on confidence and stressed about how they should introduce themselves to people out there or how they should initiate any sort of conversation, which has led them to experience social anxiety, and therefore, they have started avoiding meeting or having a conversation with people.

However, both of them are very much comfortable in their own skin. They are very fluent in their native languages, but the necessity of learning and using English has been felt by them. As English is a global language, it may not define how knowledgeable you are, but it has become mandatory to learn it.

- _This is how you do it_:

Way 1:
Hello, I am Vikas, born and brought up in New Delhi, India. I have completed my education from XYZ college, New Delhi. Cricket and reading interest me a lot. I aspire to become a sportsperson, and players such as MS Dhoni and Sachin Tendulkar inspire me. I am passionate about writing, and in time to come, I would like to publish my own book.

Way 2:
Hello, my name is Prateek, and I am from Bengaluru, Karnataka. I am a software engineer who has graduated from XYZ college, Bengaluru, and currently pursuing my dream job. I am a technophile, and exploring the unexplored areas in technology interests me a lot. Elon Musk inspires me, and I aspire to be somewhere near.

Way 3:
Hey, I am Gaurav, and I hail from Bikaner, Rajasthan. I am a lawyer by profession and a writer by passion. I have completed my degree from XYZ university, Ludhiana. I am a bibliophile and currently working on the manuscript of my first book. Mrs. Sudha Murty inspires me a lot, and I aspire to be one of the best writers in the coming future.

Interests/Hobbies:

This is a revelation that might shock you. The word "Hobbies" is never used in a conversation. It might appear in some texts, but while having a conversation, "Hobbies" is never used.

So, here you will be introduced to some attractive ways that will help you to replace "hobbies" in your daily conversations.

Introducing oneself in a formal or informal way does include mentioning one's interests. But discussing in the same old way about one's hobbies is so last season now.

Let's look at some of the ways to make your conversation a lot more captivating.

1. Cricket interests me a lot.
2. I am keen about reading.
3. I am a musicophile.
4. I love to watch movies.
5. When I have time, I usually meet up with my friends.

So, the next time someone asks you: "What are your hobbies?" just do not start with "My hobbies are ..." Instead, give them a fascinating reply.

Now, the question arises: if the word "Hobbies" is not used in a conversation, then are there any other ways to ask about someone's hobbies without using the word?

The answer to this question is definitely a Yes ...

There are a number of interesting ways you can elevate your conversation and ask someone about their interests or hobbies without using THE WORD.

- *Let's have a look at them:*

Informal Ways:

1. What do you like to do in your free time?
2. What is your go-to activity?
3. What makes your day lighten?
4. What are your favorite distractions?
5. What is your fun fix?
6. What makes your lazy day entertaining?
7. What helps your break through an unproductive day?
8. What is your idea of a well-spent day?
9. What are your interests?

Formal Ways:

1. What are your interests outside work?
2. What in your idea are leisure pursuits?
3. What do you do in your spare time?
4. How do you prefer to spend your leisure time?
5. How do you unwind?
6. What are your interests?
7. Any interests outside work?
8. Any passions?
9. How do you like to spend your weekends?

Trait Nouns:

Every person in this world is born with distinctive traits, and in order to present themselves as what they are, the use of certain Nouns are a must.

Let's have a look at what are the Nouns for the most common personality traits.

Nouns traits are the characteristics or qualities that make a person stand out.

1. **_A person who sleeps a lot:_**

A Sleepyhead

2. ***<u>A person who eats a lot:</u>***

<u>A Foodie</u>

3. ***<u>A person who talks too much:</u>***

<u>Blabbermouth</u>
Or in an informal way:
<u>Chatty</u>

4. ***<u>A person who loves to watch movies:</u>***

<u>A Cinephile</u>
Or in a more informal way:
<u>A Film Buff</u>

5. ***<u>A person who loves music:</u>***

<u>A Melophile</u>
Or in an informal way:
<u>A Music Fanatic</u>

6. ***A person who always thinks positive:***

An Optimist

7. ***A person who knows many languages:***

A Polyglot

8. ___A person who is interested in the science of language:___

A Linguist

9. ___A person who drinks alcohol regularly:___

An Alcoholic
Or in an informal way
A Drunkard or a Boozer

Note: Alcoholic can also be used for a person who is addicted to alcohol.

10. ***A person who doesn't drink at all:***

A teetotaler

Similar to these, there are many more trait nouns. Let's check them next:

Personality Trait	Trait Noun
A. A person who loves the moon	A Selenophile
B. A person who is scared of heights	An Acrophobic
C. A person who is scared of water	Aquaphobic
D. A person who doesn't believe in God	An Atheist
E. A person who lives a simple life in a monastery, away from the usual life	A Monk (Male) A Nun (Female)
F. A person who reads a lot	A Bookworm Or A Bibliophile
G. A person who has only intellectual pursuits	A Nerd
H. A person who is unusually intelligent	A Prodigy
I. A person who loves to exercise	A Fitness-Enthusiast
J. A person who does something bad to bring disgrace to a family or a group	A Black Sheep
K. A person who steals as a habit	A Kleptomaniac
L. A stupid person	A Blockhead
M. A child who behaves badly	A Brat
N. An obsequious person	A Brown Nose
O. A person who flatters the powerful	A Sycophant or an Obsequious person
P. A person who does silly things to make others laugh	A Buffoon (Clown)

Q. A person who enjoys seeing others in pain	A Sadist
R. A person who insults or threatens people weaker than him	A Bully
S. A person who tends to drop things or is careless	Clumsy
T. A person for whom their career is the only priority	A Careerist
U. A person who favors some over others	A Biased Person
V. A person who intends to do bad to others or who backbites	A Malevolent
W. A person who travels a lot	A Traveler or a Voyager
X. A person who loves traveling	A Hodophile
Y. A person who does not spend much	A Miser or a Cheapskate
Z. A person who spends a lot	A Spendthrift
AA. A person who believes that women are less important than men	A Chauvinist
BB. A person who has nice handwriting	A Calligraphist
CC. A person who can't decide anything	Indecisive
DD. A person who creates a facade to seek attention	Histrionic
EE. A person who has no courage or gets scared in difficult situations	A Coward
FF. A person who cries or complains very often, even at smallest of things	A Crybaby

GG. A dishonest person or a criminal	A Crook
HH. A person who is blamed for an offence	An Accused
II. A person who believes other people help only for some motive	A Cynic
JJ. A person who thinks of being somewhere or with someone rather than living in the moment	A Daydreamer
KK. A person who is always before time (arrives, rises, or acts before the usual time)	An Early Bird
LL. A person who listens to someone's private conversations without them knowing of it	An Eavesdropper
MM. A person who has extreme political opinions	An Extremist
NN. A person who is very crazy and enthusiastic about something	A Fanatic
OO. A person who dresses very fashionably	A Fashion Plate
PP. A person who is very deeply involved in something	A Freak
QQ. A person who works a lot (with either negative or positive feelings)	A Workaholic
RR. A person who shops a lot or who loves to shop	A Shopaholic
SS. A stupid person	An Airhead

This table gives us the Noun Traits for the different people around us. We all must have been around such people by-and-by, but little did we know that there are Nouns to describe them.

Like traits, there are people around us, and even we ourselves, who show some feelings that we can't generally define in just a word. Let's look at some of our feelings that show our interests in and around us.

Feelings	Nouns
A cat lover	An Ailurophile
A person who loves flowers	An Anthophile
A person who collects teddy bears	An Arctophile
A person who loves stars and astronomy	An Astrophile
A person who loves being alone	An Autophile
A person who loves books and collects them	A Bibliophile
A person who loves cold weather and snow	A Chionophile
A dog lover	A Cynophile
A person who loves trees and forests	A Dendrophile
A person who is happy to work for longer periods	An Ergophile
A lover of the sun	A Heliophile
A person who loves to drink coffee	A Javaphile
A person who loves words	A Logophile
A person who loves shade or darkness	A Nyctophile
A person who loves rain	A Pluviophile
A person who loves sunsets	An Opacarophile
A person who loves clouds	A Nephophile
A person who loves the moon	Selenophile

After knowing a lot about the nouns based on our traits and feelings, let's have a look at the adjectives that also tell us how a person is in terms of behavior and actions.

PERSONALITY ADJECTIVES:

The specific words that are used to define a person's personality and behavior toward other people:

POSITIVE	NEGATIVE
Affable, Amiable, Amicable (a person who is friendly and pleasant)	**Abrasive (a rude and harsh person)**
Brave (a person who isn't scared of anything)	**Aggressive (a person who loses his temper easily)**
Calm (a person who isn't aggressive and loud)	**Apathetic (a person who is low on enthusiasm or is not interested in anything)**
Cheerful (a person who is always happy)	**Aloof (an unfriendly person)**
Charming (a person who has an attractive personality)	**Anxious (a person who panics in difficult situations)**

Compassionate (a person who is empathetic toward people)	**Arrogant (a person who thinks superior of himself because of his abilities)**
Circumspective, Calculative. (a person who judges a situation carefully before acting on it)	**Boisterous (a very loud and noisy person)**
Courteous (a person who is polite and mannerly)	**Bossy (a person who instructs everyone what to do)**
Creative (a person who has new ideas or ways of doing different things)	**Belligerent (an aggressive person)**
Charismatic (a person with an attractive and influential personality)	**Boastful (a person who shows off his achievements a lot)**
Convivial (a person who has a pleasant and friendly nature)	**Big-headed (an arrogant person)**
Diligent (a person who puts efforts in work and duty)	**Callous (a person who shows no sympathy toward anyone)**

Determined (a person who is firm on decisions to achieve success)	Cynical (a person who does not trust the intentions of any other person and believes that they are only interested in themselves)
Diplomatic (a person who controls an unpleasant situation without upsetting anyone)	Clingy (a person who gets attached to people too much and depends on them emotionally)
Empathetic (a person who can relate and feel what others are feeling)	Confrontational (a person who deals with situations aggressively)
Efficient (a person who performs in the best way without wasting time and resources)	Cowardly (a person who is not brave and tries to avoid danger of any kind)
Enthusiastic (a person who is very much interested in some activity and spends a lot of time on it)	Deceitful (a person who is dishonest and makes others believe in things that are not true)
Exuberant (a person who is very energetic and full of cheerfulness)	Defensive (a person who always justifies himself to be correct and cannot take any criticism)

Faithful (a person who always supports and is honest)	**Devious (a person who tends to lie and trick people; usually a person with devil qualities)**
Fearless (a person who does not fear anything)	**Dim (a slow learner or a person who lacks intellectual acuteness)**
Friendly (a person who makes you feel comfortable)	**Domineering (a person who has the tendency to control other people)**
Funny (a person who has a good sense of humor)	**Egotistical (a person who has an exaggerated sense of self-importance)**
Generous (a person who is liberal in helping people, mostly in monetary terms)	**Finicky, Fussy (a person who is very difficult to please)**
Gentle (a person who is sensitive toward other people's feelings)	**Fanatic (a person who is excessively interested in something that it is beyond limits)**
Gregarious (a person who likes to meet people)	**Gussy (a person who dresses up in a very attractive way for attention)**

Honest (a person who does not lie)	**Gullible (a person who easily believes what others say)**
Humorous (a person who is funny)	**Grumpy (a person who gets cranky or irritable easily)**
Imaginative (a person who has good ideas)	**Impatient (a person who gets easily irritated and restless, or a person who cannot wait long)**
Intuitive (a person who can presume something before it actually happens)	**Impulsive (a person who takes decisions in the heat of the moment without being calculative)**
Intellectual (a person who is very intelligent)	**Inconsiderate (a person who is thoughtless about others)**
Inventive (a person who is good at making unique and unusual things)	**Ignorant (a person who is lacking the knowledge of certain things)**
Kooky (a person who is crazily interesting)	**Indecisive (a person who finds it difficult to make decisions)**

Laid-back (a person who is always relaxed)	Inconsiderate (a person who doesn't care about others' feelings)
Magnanimous (a person who is very kind and generous)	Intolerant (a person who does not accept others' opinions)
Optimistic (a person who has a positive mindset)	Irresponsible (a person who is careless about the work given to him)
Passionate (a person who has strong beliefs in something)	Loud (a person who has a very loud voice and is overconfident)
Plucky (a courageous person)	Mean (a person who just thinks of himself)
Polite (a humble person)	Moody (a person whose moods change frequently)
Placid (a person who is calm by nature and does not easily get impulsive)	Narrow-minded (a person who is unwilling to accept new ideas and is rigid about his thinking)

Pioneering (a person who becomes the first person to do something)	Nasty (a person whose behavior is unpleasant and bad)
Philosophical (a person who lives by a certain idea, wonder, or reason)	Obstinate (a person who is rigid or inflexible about perspectives)
Persistent (a person who sticks to the task even when the situation gets tough)	Overcritical (a person who points out faults very often and in everything)
Rational (a person who is practical about situations)	Patronizing (a person who shows a superior attitude toward others)
Realistic (a person who is well aware of the reality)	Pigheaded (a person who is stubborn in changing his mind even when it is in his or her best interest)
Resourceful (a person who has good connections)	Pessimistic (a person who has negative thinking)
Romantic (a person who is lovable and loving)	Pompous (an arrogant person or a person with a huge ego)

Reliable (a person one can depend on)	**Possessive (a person who wants the attention of his or her loved ones all by themselves)**
Resilient (a person who can get out of an unfavorable situation easily)	**Resentful (a person who behaves bitterly because he is forced to accept something he doesn't like)**
Sensible (a logical person)	**Secretive (a person who hides his or her emotions, intentions, and motives from others)**
Sincere (a person who is genuine)	**Stubborn (a person who resists any kind of change)**
Sociable (a person who likes to meet people)	**Sneaky (a person who is very secretive)**
Sympathetic (a person who shows concern for people in bad situations)	**Sullen (a person who has a bad temper and is very sulky)**
Timid (a person who is a coward)	**Snarky (a person who has a rude and sarcastic tone)**

Thoughtful (a person who is concerned about others' feelings)	**Tactless (a person who is insensitive toward others)**
Upbeat (a person who is hopeful and cheerful)	**Thoughtless (a person who is not sympathetic toward people)**
Unassuming (a person who is quiet and doesn't like too much attention)	**Unpredictable (a person whose actions are unknown)**
Versatile (a person who is an all-rounder and has multiple skills)	**Unreliable (a person who cannot be trusted with important tasks)**
Warm-hearted (a person who is kind and sympathetic)	**Untrustworthy (a person who cannot be trusted)**
Wise (a person who can guide and treat people according to his or her abilities)	**Vague (a person who is unclear of his or her actions)**
Witty (a person who has an intelligent sense of humor)	**Vain (a person who is extremely proud of his or her appearance or achievements)**
	Weak-willed (a person who can be easily manipulated)

II
Chapter 2: Daily Conversations

Meeting and talking with people in our daily life is something, as humans, we enjoy a lot. But aren't there are instances when we do feel diffident or clueless about how to initiate a conversation or even how to reply to a question?

We do sometimes! Let's take a look at some of the common daily conversations that we come across frequently.

How to Know About Someone's Well-being and Whereabouts and How to Reply to Them

- Hey, how are you? (आप कैसे हैं?)

  I am good. Thank you! How about you? (मैं अच्छी हु| धन्यवाद| आप कैसे हैं?)

- Hello, where have you been? (तुम कहा थे?)

  I was busy with some stuff. What about you? (मैं कुछ कामो में व्यसत थी| और आप?)

- Hey, where have you been all this time? (तुम इतने समय से कहा थे?)

I was right here. (मैं यही थी।)
or
I was caught up with some stuff. (मैं कुछ कामो में उलझी हुई थी।)

- How have you been? (तुम कैसे थे?)

I have been great. Thank you! How about you? (मैं बहुत अच्छी रही। धन्यवाद! आप कैसे थे?)

- How are you doing? (आप कैसे हो?)

I am doing good. Thank you! What about you? (मेरा सब अच्छा चल रहा हैं धन्यवाद! आप बताइए।)

- Hey, long time no see. (बहुत समय बाद मिलना हुआ.)

Yes, it's been ages. How have you been? (हा, काफी समय हो गया। तुम कैसे थे?)

- What are you up to these days? (आज कल क्या कर रहे हो?)

Nothing much, just busy with some projects. (ज्यादा कुछ नहीं, बस कुछ काम में लगी हूँ।)
or
Working on my health these days. (अपनी सेहत पर ध्यान दे रही हूँ आज कल।)
or
Nothing much, down with fever. (कुछ नहीं, मुझे बुखार हो रखा हैं)

- What's brewing? (क्या खिचड़ी पक रही हैं?)

Something you would love to read/eat/watch/play/experience! (कुछ ऐसा लेख/ खाना/ मूवी या खेल जो तुम्हे बहुत पसंद आने वाला हैं)
It's a surprise for you! (यह तुम्हारे लिए एक तोहफा होगा।)
Planning for a happening event! (एक बड़े उत्सव की तैयारी हो रही हैं)

Planning for a night sneak-out! (रात को चुपके से निकलने की तैयारी।)

- What is up with you? (क्या हो गया है तुम्हें?)

I am not feeling myself today! (मुझे कुछ अच्छा नहीं लग रहा है।)
I am feeling anxious. (मुझे घबराहट हो रही है।)
I am not in my skin today. (मुझे यहाँ आराम नहीं मिल रहा है।)
I am not in a good mood. (मेरा मूड ठीक नहीं है।)
I am not in the mood to talk. (मेरा बात करने का मन नहीं है।)

Conversations When You Have Guests at Your Home:

- Hey, come on in. Good to see you. (नमस्ते, अन्दर आइये। आपको देख के खुशी हुई।)
- I hope it wasn't a trouble reaching here/finding my house. (आशा करती हूं की आपको घर मिलने में कोई तकलीफ नहीं हुई।)
- Consider this as your home. (इसे अपना ही घर समझिये।) (Beginner level)

Make yourself comfortable. (Moderate level)
Please make yourself at home. (Advanced level)

- How have you been? (कैसे थे आप?)
- What would you like to have? (आप क्या लेना पसंद करेंगे?)
- How did you like the food/drinks? (आपको खाना/पेय पदार्थ कैसे लगे?)
- It was great to have you here. Hoping to hang out again soon. (आप आये बहुत अच्छा लगा। आशा करती हूं जल्दी ही वापस मिलेंगे।)
- Drive safely/reach safely/ping me once you reach. (ध्यान से जाना/ पहुंच के बता देना।)

- *When you are a guest:*

- Hi, how are you? (नमस्ते, आप कैसे हैं?)
- I hope we are on time. (if you are there for some occasion) (आशा करती हूं हम समय पर आये हैं।)

- You have a beautiful house. (Beginner level)

  Your house is spectacular. (Moderate level)
  You have exquisite interiors. (Advanced level)
  (आपका घर बहुत सुन्दर हैं / आपने घर को बहुत सुन्दर सजाया हैं)
  Note: Pronunciation of Exquisite: **X-Q-Sit.**
  Pronunciation of Spectacular: **Spec-tac-Q-lar.**

- Where is the bathroom? (Beginner level)

  Where is the washroom? (Moderate level)
  Which way is the loo/washroom? (Advanced level)
  (वाशरूम किस तरफ है?)

- I would like to have some tea/juice/coffee with no added sugar. (मैं चाय/
  ज्यूस/ कॉफ़ी लूंगी बिना चीनी को)
- The food was amazing. (Beginner level)

  The food was delicious. (Moderate level)
  The food was delectable. (Advanced level)
  (खाना बहुत स्वादिष्ट था| / पेय पदार्थ ताजगी से भरे थे|)

- I enjoyed it a lot. Let's meet again soon. (Beginner level)

  I had fun. Let's plan and meet soon. (Moderate level)
  I had a great time here. Let's plan an evening soon. (Advanced level)
  (मुझे यहाँ बहुत मज़ा आया| जल्दी एक शाम और मिलते हैं|)

- It's too late, I should go now. (Beginner level)

  It's really late, I should take your leave now. (Moderate level)
  It's beyond late. I should dash. (Advanced level)
  (बहुत देर हो गयी हैं अब मुझे जाना चाहिए|)

When You Meet Someone for the First Time:

The first thing to do when we meet someone for the very first time is to ask their name. "What is your name?" is the basic question that we have learnt to ask all our lives. And that is good to go, but there are certain other ways that you may use to ask someone's name.

Here are they:

a. May I know your name?
b. What should I call you?
c. What can I call you?
d. Do you mind if I ask you your name?
e. What was your name you said?
f. Please remind me of your name.
g. Can I have your name?

- *Common answers to the above questions:*

I. I am Sonia.
II. My name is Sonia.
III. You can call me Sonia.
IV. It's Sonia for you.
V. Sure, I am Sonia.

III

Chapter 3: General Conversations

Let's take you on a ride and make you familiar with all the **advanced forms** of the **common conversations** that are a part of our daily life.

1. Pay attention to what he is saying: Pay heed to what he is saying. (ध्यान दो, वो क्या बोल रहा है।)

2. I had a bad dream: I had a nightmare. (मुझे एक बुरा सपना आया।)

Note: Never use the word "SEE" for dreams, as it is used for the things that you see with your eyes open.

1. Don't irritate me: I have had enough of you. (मुझे परेशान मत करो।)

2. I am going to take bath: I am going to take a shower. (मैं नहाने जा रही हूँ।)

3. I am going out: I am heading out. (मैं बाहर जा रही हूँ।)

4. I talked to her: I had a word with her. (मेरी उससे बात हुई।)

5. We had a little talk: We had a little conversation. (हमारी थोड़ी बात हुई।)

6. I want the seat next to the window seat in the plane: I want the aisle seat. (मुझे हवाई जहाज की आइल सीट चाहिए।)

7. Why is there so much garbage here?: Why is this place littered? (यहाँ इतना कचरा क्यूँ है?)

8. Clean the garbage: Clean the litter. (कचरा साफ़ करो।)

9. Vicky threw garbage in the room: Vicky littered the room. (विक्की ने कमरे में कचरा कयिा।)

10. I want water to stop my thirst: I want water to quench my thirst. (मुझे पानी चाहिए प्यास बुझाने के लिए।)

11. I had a bad dream: I had a nightmare. (मुझे एक बुरा सपना आया।)

12. I have to go: I got to dash. (मुझे जाना पड़ेगा।)

13. Please get the bill: Please get the check. (कृपया बिल ले आईये।)

14. You're welcome: Anytime, or don't mention it, or glad to help, or the pleasure is all mine. (मुझे ख़ुशी हुई।)

15. I am hungry: I am famished.(मुझे बूख लगी है।)

16. I am tired: I am exhausted. (मैं बहुत थकी हुई हूँ।)

17. She ditched me: She betrayed me, or she deceived me. (उसने मुझे धोका दिया।)

18. I love to sleep: I am a sleepyhead. (मुझे सोना पसन्द है।)

19. I love sweets: I have a sweet tooth. (मुझे मीठा खाना पसंद है।)

20. You have worn your T-shirt wrong: You have worn your T-shirt inside out or back to front. (तुमने टी-शर्ट उल्टी पहनी है।)

21. This dress is short for you now: You have outgrown this dress. (ये ड्रेस तुम्हे छोट्टी हो गयी है।)

22. Could you help me?: Could you give me a hand?/Do you mind doing this for me? (क्या तुम मेरी मदद करोगे?)

23. She was laughing at me in front of others: She made fun of me/She mocked me. (उसने मेरा मजाक बनाया।)

24. It is very easy: It is not rocket science. (ये बहुत सरल है।)

25. Keep me informed: Keep me in loop. (मुझे बताते रहिएगा।)

26. Stay in touch: Don't be a stranger. (संपर्क में रहिएगा।)

27. I don't like math/I am not good in math: I am bad at math. (मेरी मैथ्स बहुत बुरी है।)

28. She stopped meeting me: She ghosted me. (उसने मुझसे मिलना ही बंद कर दिया।)

29. I don't believe it: I don't buy that. (मुझे इसपे विश्वास नहीं है।)

30. Tell me the gossip: Spill the beans. (भेद खोलदो।)

31. Don't ignore me: Don't turn your back on me. (मुझसे मुँह मत मोड़ो।)

32. She wakes up early: She is an early bird. (वो सुबह जल्दी उठती है।)

33. She sleeps late at night: She is a night owl. (वो रात को देर से सोती है।)

34. She is very dramatic: She is histrionic. (वो बहुत नाटक करती है।)

35. My exams are almost here: My exams are around the corner. (मेरी परीक्षा आने वाली है।)

36. Lock the door: Latch the door. (दरवाज़े की कुण्डी लगा दो।)

37. A statue of Ravan is burnt on Dussehra: An effigy of Ravan is burnt on Dussehra. (दशरे पर रावन का पुतला जलाया जाता है।)

38. I don't agree with you: I beg to differ. (मैं तुमसे सहमत नहीं हूँ।)

39. It is kind of impossible: When pigs fly. (यह नामुमकिन है।)

Let's take you on a ride and make you familiar with all the **advanced forms** of the **common conversations** that are a part of our daily life.

1. Pay attention to what he is saying: Pay heed to what he is saying. (ध्यान दो, वो क्या बोल रहा है।)

2. I had a bad dream: I had a nightmare. (मुझे एक बुरा सपना आया।)

Note: Never use the word "SEE" for dreams, as it is used for the things that you see with your eyes open.

1. Don't irritate me: I have had enough of you. (मुझे परेशा मत करो।)

2. I am going to take bath: I am going to take a shower. (मैं नहाने जा रही हूँ।)

3. I am going out: I am heading out. (मैं बाहर जा रही हूँ।)

4. I talked to her: I had a word with her. (मेरी उससे बात हुई।)

5. We had a little talk: We had a little conversation. (हमारी थोड़ी बात हुई।)

6. I want the seat next to the window seat in the plane: I want the aisle seat. (मुझे हवाई जहाज की आइल सीट चाहिए।)

7. Why is there so much garbage here?: Why is this place littered? (यहाँ इतना कचरा क्यूँ है?)

8. Clean the garbage: Clean the litter. (कचरा साफ़ करो।)

9. Vicky threw garbage in the room: Vicky littered the room. (विक्की ने कमरे में कचरा किया।)

10. I want water to stop my thirst: I want water to quench my thirst. (मुझे पानी चाहिए प्यास बुझाने के लिए।)

11. I had a bad dream: I had a nightmare. (मुझे एक बुरा सपना आया।)

12. I have to go: I got to dash. (मुझे जाना पड़ेगा।)

13. Please get the bill: Please get the check. (कृपया बिल ले आईये।)

14. You're welcome: Anytime, or don't mention it, or glad to help, or the pleasure is all mine. (मुझे ख़ुशी हुई।)

15. I am hungry: I am famished.(मुझे बूख लगी है।)

16. I am tired: I am exhausted. (मैं बहुत थकी हुई हूँ।)

17. She ditched me: She betrayed me, or she deceived me. (उसने मुझे धोका दिया।)

18. I love to sleep: I am a sleepyhead. (मुझे सोना पसन्द है।)

19. I love sweets: I have a sweet tooth. (मुझे मीठा खाना पसंद है।)

20. You have worn your T-shirt wrong: You have worn your T-shirt inside out or back to front. (तुमने टी-शर्ट उल्टी पहेनी है।)

21. This dress is short for you now: You have outgrown this dress. (ये ड्रेस तुम्हे छोट्टी हो गयी है।)

22. Could you help me?: Could you give me a hand?/Do you mind doing this for me? (क्या तुम मेरी मदद करोगे?)

23. She was laughing at me in front of others: She made fun of me/She mocked me. (उसने मेरा मजाक बनाया।)

24. It is very easy: It is not rocket science. (ये बहुत सरल है।)

25. Keep me informed: Keep me in loop. (मुझे बताते रहिएगा।)

26. Stay in touch: Don't be a stranger. (संपर्क में रहिएगा।)

27. I don't like math/I am not good in math: I am bad at math. (मेरी मैथ्स बहुत बुरी है।)

28. She stopped meeting me: She ghosted me. (उसने मुझसे मिलना ही बंद कर दिया।)

29. I don't believe it: I don't buy that. (मुझे इसपे विश्वास नहीं है।)

30. Tell me the gossip: Spill the beans. (भेद खोलदो।)

31. Don't ignore me: Don't turn your back on me. (मुझसे मुँह मत मोड़ो।)

32. She wakes up early: She is an early bird. (वो सुबह जल्दी उठती है।)

33. She sleeps late at night: She is a night owl. (वो रात को देर से सोती है।)

34. She is very dramatic: She is histrionic. (वो बहुत नाटक करती है।)

35. My exams are almost here: My exams are around the corner. (मेरी परीक्षा आने वाली है।)

36. Lock the door: Latch the door. (दरवाज़े की कुण्डी लगा दो।)

37. A statue of Ravan is burnt on Dussehra: An effigy of Ravan is burnt on Dussehra. (दशरे पर रावन का पुतला जलाया जाता है।)

38. I don't agree with you: I beg to differ. (मैं तुमसे सहमत नहीं हूँ।)

39. It is kind of impossible: When pigs fly. (यह नामुमकिन है।)

IV
Chapter 4: Make Your Conversations Interesting with Idioms

How many times a day do we make our conversations sound fancy through the use of Hindi idioms and phrases? Quite a lot, but do we know how to use them while conversing in English?

Let's take a look and learn some cool idioms to make our conversation fancy.

Frequently Used Idioms to Enhance Your Communication:

- मेरी आँखो का तारा|: Apple of my eyes
- एक ही थाली के चट्ट बट्टो|: Birds of the same feather flock together
- जतिना ज़्यादा उतना अच्छा|: The more the merrier
- दूर के ढोल सुहावनो|: The grass is always greener on the other side.
- एक हाथ से ताली नही बजती|: It takes two to tango.
- अपने मुँह मियां मट्ठू बनना|: To blow one's own trumpet
- तुम्हारे मुँह में घी शक्कर|: May God bless your words.
- सीधे बात पर आओ|: Cut to the chase

- बातें मत घुमाओ|: Stop beating around the bush.
- चिंता मत करो|: Don't sweat it.
- नाच न जाने आंगन टेढ़ा|: A bad workman quarrels with his tools.
- दोनों हाथो में लड्डू: Best of both the worlds.
- जो होना है वो ही होगा|: What's meant to happen will happen.
- सालो में कभी एक बार|: Once in a blue moon
- हर कोने- कोने में|: In every nook and cranny
- ऊँट के मुह में जीरा|: A drop in the ocean
- नज़र लगाना|: To cast an evil eye
- कान खोलकर सुनना|: To be all ears
- नज़र उतारना|: To cast off an evil eye
- थोथा चना, बाजे घना|: Empty vessels sound much.
- जो गरजते है वो बरसते नही|: Barking dogs seldom bite.
- अंत भला तो सब भला|: All is well that ends well.
- बगल में छोरा, शहर में ढींढोरा: Right under the nose
- डूबते को तिनके का सहारा|: Grasping at straws
- अब पछताए होत क्या, जब चिड़िया चुग गयी खेत|: Don't cry over spilled milk.
- लोहे के चने चबाना|: A hard nut to crack
- चोर की दाड़ी में तिनका|: A guilty conscience needs no accuser.
- शैतान का नाम लिया और शैतान हाज़िर|: Think of the devil and the devil appears.
- आग में घी डालना|: Add fuel to fire.
- जैसा करोगे, वैसा भरोगे|: As you sow, so shall you reap.
- उम्मीद पर दुनिया कायम है|: Hope sustains life.
- जहा निराशा वहा आशा|: Every dark cloud has a silver lining.
- राई का पहाड़ बनाना|: To make a mountain out of a molehill.
- जहा चाह, वहा राह|: Where there is a will, there is a way.
- सब्र का फल मीठा होता है|: Patience bears sweet fruits.
- दुःख के भेष में सुख|: A blessing in disguise
- जो हो गया सो हो गया|: Let bygones be bygones.
- अन्धो में काणा राजा|: A figure among ciphers
- एक पंथ दो काज|: To kill two birds with one stone
- हवाई महल बनाना|: To build a castle in the air
- ऊँची दुकान फीके पकवान|: Great boast, little roast

- एक मछली सारे तालाब को गंदा कर देती है।: A black sheep infects the whole flock.
- दुःख के भेष में सुख।: A blessing in disguise

V

Chapter 5: Improve Your Daily Conversation Skills

Our daily life revolves around our home, school, and restaurants here and there. We do sometimes hesitate in initiating and replying to certain questions, and as a result, we avoid being a part of the conversation.

Here we have a few ideas to initiate, indulge, and be a part of the conversation going around. Let's take a look.

School Conversations:

- *For students:*

- Greet the teacher whenever you come across them. Always greet the teacher with a pleasant smile.

Good morning, ma'am, and good afternoon, ma'am.

- Whenever you want the teacher to repeat something for you:

a. Could you please repeat it for me, ma'am? (Beginner level)

b. I couldn't hear you. Could you please repeat it, ma'am? (Moderate level)
c. Ma'am, could you pardon me? (Advanced level)

Note: Never request or ask someone using the word **"Can,"** because **"Can"** indicates the capability of a person. Every person is capable of doing everything, but when you seek permission, you are asking the other person to allow you. So always start with **"May"** or **"Could,"** accordingly.

Always raise your hand first before you ask anything from the teacher in the middle of a class.

When a teacher has asked you to call someone from the other class or get a book or a notebook from the other section or make some important announcement:

You go to the other class and converse in the following way:

- May I come in, ma'am? (Never stretch your hand out while asking this.)

When you have an announcement to make:

- I have an announcement to make, may I?

When a teacher asks you to call a student from another class:

- Sonia Ma'am has called for Jayshree.

When a teacher asks you to get a book or a notebook from another class:

- Gemini Ma'am is asking for a science book/notebook.

When you need to converse with your fellow mates regarding certain things such as:

- When you want to borrow something:

Could you help me with a pen/pencil/ruler/eraser?
Certain situations you need to take care of:

- Never yawn with your mouth wide open. Always cover your mouth with your hand.

If a teacher is in the middle of a conversation/explanation, and you want her permission to drink water or go to the washroom, the following should be the right way to seek permission:

a. Raise your hand

Then wait for the teacher to address your request and allow you to speak:

a. Stand up from your seat and ask:

· May I drink water? (Beginner level)

May I have water? (Advanced level)

· May I go to the washroom? (Beginner level)

May I use the loo? (Advanced level)

· *For teachers:*

Even teachers do face trouble in framing the right question to ask the students in certain situations. And as a teacher, it is not appreciated to use incorrect English language. Let's see some of the examples:

· **When a student has been absent for many days:**

Why were you on leave for so long? (तुम इतने दिन छुट्टी पर क्यों थे?)

· **When you have to ask whether they have completed their work or not:**

Did you all finish your work? (क्या तुम सबने अपना काम खत्म कर लिया?)

· **When you want to know who has not completed their work:**

How many of you have not done your work? (तुम में से किस किस ने अपना काम नहीं पूरा किया?)

- **When a student comes very late from the washroom or from somewhere you sent them for some work:**

What took you so long? (तुम्हे इतनी दरे कैसे लग गई?)

- **When you want to send a student to the other class to bring a book from there:**

Could you go and get me a book from the other section? (क्या तुम दूसरी कक्षा से जा कर मरे लिए एक बुक ला दोगे?)

- **When you want to know who wants to take part in the annual function:**

Who all are interested in participating in the annual function? (कोन कोन वार्षकि उत्सव में भाग लेना चाहता है?)

- **When you want to call a student from the other class:**

Could you please go and call Jayshree from section A? (क्या तुम भाग अ से जयश्री को बुला लाओगे?)

- **When you want to know who have not completed their test:**

How many of you are yet to complete your test? (तुम में से कसि कसि की परीक्षा पूरी होना बाकि है?)

- **When you want to know if the students have prepared for the test:**

Have you all prepared for the test? (क्या तुम सबने कक्षा परीक्षा की तैयारी करी है?)

- **When you want to know the marks of the students :**

How much did you score? (तुम्हरे कतिने अंक आए?)

- **When you want to meet a student's parents:**

I want you to call your parents tomorrow to the school. (तुम कल तुम्हारे माता पतिा को स्कूल लेके आना!)

<u>Restaurant Conversations:</u>

<u>Questions generally asked:</u>
<u>By the staff to the customer:</u>
The staff will always greet the customer first and make them feel welcomed.
Always start with:
Hello, sir, welcome.
And then ask them if they have already reserved a table or not:

i. Do you have any reservations? (क्या आपने टेबल बुक करवाई थी?)

ii. You have a reservation under what name? (आपकी टेबल कसि नाम से बुक करवाई थी?)

Make a table available for them, provide them with the menu card, and then ask:

iii. What would you like to have? (आप क्या लेना पसंद करेंगे?)

iv. What would you prefer? Bottled water, normal water, or sparkling water? (आप कैसा पानी लेंगे: बोतल वाला, सादा पानी या स्पर्क्लगि पानी।)

(एक पानी की बोतल ले आइयो।)
After the guests are finished with their meal, then ask:

v. How did you like the food? (आपको खाना कैसा लगा?)

After the guests have reviewed the food, ask if they want anything else:

vi. Anything else you need, sir?

If the answer is yes, provide them with the order, and if the answer is no, then ask:

vii. How would you like to pay? Cash or card? (Beginner level)

What would be your preferred mode of payment? Cash or card? (Advanced level)

(आप कैसे बिल चुकायेंगे?)

- *A conversation between the customer and the restaurant staff:*

Staff: Welcome, sir/ma'am. Do you have any reservations?

Customer: Hello, we have booked a table for two by the name of Mr. and Mrs. Chopra. (Beginner level)

OR

Hello, we have a reservation under the name of Mr. and Mrs. Chopra. (Advanced level)

(हमने एक टेबल बुक करवाई है, श्रीमती और श्री चोपड़ा के नाम से।)

Once the staff confirms the reservation and makes the guests seated:

Staff: Here's the menu, sir. What would you like to order?/What would you like to have?

Customer: Give us a minute and we will let you know.

(हमें थोडा वक़्त दीजिये, हम बताते हैं।)

What is the best dish of your restaurant/hotel? (Beginner level)

What is your specialty? (Moderate level)

What is the chef's specialty? (Advanced level)

(आपके यहाँ क्या अच्छा मिलता है?)

OR

Please suggest some good food options to try.

(कोई अच्छी डिश सुझाइए।)

Staff: Sir, you can go for Italian, especially the chef's special pizza.

(आप इटालियन ले सकते हैं, खास कर के पिज़्ज़ा।)

Customer: What all cuisines do you offer?

(आपके पास कौन कौन से तरह के व्यंजन हैं?)

Staff: We have Italian, Indian, Mexican, Mughlai, and Chinese cuisines.

(हमारे पास इटालियन, मेक्सिकन, इंडियन, मुघलई और चीनी खाना मिलता है।)

Customer: I want to order Indian. (Beginner level)

Or

I would like to order Indian. (Moderate level)

Or

I would like to have Indian. (Advanced level)

(मैं इंडियन खाना लेना पसंद करूँगा।)

Once the order is placed, the following conversations are initiated:

i. Staff: How was the food, sir? (Beginner level)

Or

Did you like the food, sir? (Moderate level)

Or

How did you like the food, sir? (Advanced level)

(आपको खाना कैसा लगा?)

Customer: The food was great. (Beginner level)

Or

The food was delicious. (Moderate level)

Or

The food was delectable. (Advanced level)

(खाना बहुत अच्छा था।)

Staff: Thank you, sir.

(धन्यवाद।)

Customer: Please bring the bill. (Beginner level)

Or

Please get the bill. (Moderate level)

Or

Please get me the check. (Advanced level)

(कृपया बिल ले आईये।)

Staff: Sure, sir. How will you pay the bill? By cash or card? (Beginner level)

Or

Sure, sir. How will you make the payment? By cash or card? (Moderate level)

Or

Sure, sir. How would you like to pay? By cash or card? (Advanced level)

(जी ज़रूर। आप बिल का भुगतान कैसे करेंगे? कैश से या कार्ड से?)

Customer: I will make the payment in cash.

Or

I will pay in cash.

Or

I would like to pay in cash.

(मैं कैश से भुगतान करना चाहूँगा।)

If the payment is to be made by card:
I will make the payment by card.

Or

I will pay by card.

Or

I would like to pay by card.
(मैं कार्ड के द्वारा भुगतान करना चाहूँगा।)

When you want to use the washroom, you can ask in the following way:
Where is the toilet? (Beginner level)

Or

Where is the washroom? (Moderate level)

Or

Which way is the washroom? (Advanced level)
(बाथरूम कहा है?)

VI

Chapter 6: Basic Rules for Fluency

Learning the grammar rules to achieve fluency in speaking English is a tiring task. There are approximately thirty-five hundred grammar rules, and acing all of them is an impossible act.

So here I bring to you a few rules that would help you to be more fluent and confident in your conversation without cramming the whopping thirty-five hundred rules of grammar.

1. Subject-Verb Agreement:

Subject	Verb
Singular	Singular
Plural	Plural

For instance:

- They like watching movie.

Subject: They (Plural)

Verb: Like (Plural)

- She likes to dance.

  Subject: She (Singular)
  Verb: Likes (Singular)
  Exception: I am taken as Plural. I dance, I drive, etc.

1. Always use the First Form of Verb with "Didn't."

   For instance:
   She didn't know who he was.
   Never use third form with didn't.
   She didn't know who he was.

3. Try and use less words to enhance your communication skills.

   For example:

- I love sleeping whenever I have some free time.

  We can write it as: I am a sleepyhead.

- I love trying different cuisines.

  We can write it as: I am a foodie.

- I don't believe in God.

  We can write it as: I am an atheist.

- She gels easily with everybody.

  We can write it as: She is an extrovert.

4. Never form the sentences in Hindi and then translate into English:

It is always believed that in order to master any language in the world, you have to befriend it. That is, you have to treat that language as your friend and try and share everything in that language. The more you get comfortable with the language by making it a part of your daily life, the better you will get at it in no time.

Before starting any conversation with anybody, always remember if you are going to have the conversation in English, you will have to think and speak simultaneously in English. Thinking in Hindi or any of your native tongues and then translating it in English is a big NO-NO.

The best tip to achieve fluency is to think and speak in English. The more you practice this, the more you will be able to become good at it.

The second thought that backs this is that English is a very friendly language. You do not have to translate every word of the sentence in Hindi or in any other language to English. Going word by word in forming sentences might mess up the idea of what you want to convey.

Let's take a look at how thinking and translating can make your conversations awkward:

- दविाली आनेवाली हौ

Translation in English: Diwali is coming.
Correct way : Diwali is around the corner.

- तमुहे ये ड्रेस छोट्टी हो गयी हौ

Translation in English: This dress has become short for you.
Correct way: You have outgrown this dress.

- तमुने ये शर्ट उल्टी पहेनी हौ

Translation in English: You have worn this shirt wrongly.
Correct way: You have worn this shirt inside out.

- तमुहे आज कैसी नींद आई?

Translation in English: How was your sleep today?
Correct way: Did you have a good sleep today?

- मैं उसे अच्छे से जानता हूँ

Translation in English: I know him good.
Correct way: I know him well.

- यह सलाद किसने बनाया है?

Translation in English: Who cooked this salad?
Correct way: Who made this salad?

- वो दिल्ली से पन्द्रह दिन पहले आई।

Translation in English: She came from Delhi fifteen days before.
Correct way: She arrived about a fortnight ago from Delhi.

- मैं पंजाब में पली बड़ी हूँ

Translation in English: I am grown and raised in Punjab.
Correct way: I was born and brought up in Punjab.

- मैं कल परीक्षा दूंगी।

Translation in English: I will give the exam tomorrow.
Correct way: I will write the exam tomorrow.

5. A negative sentence should end with a positive question and vice versa.

   For example:
   <u>You did not complete your work, did you?</u>
   A negative sentence. A positive question.
   Similarly,
   <u>You did complete your project, didn't you?</u>
   A positive sentence. A negative question.

6. How to answer to the questions starting with:

   Do, Did, Will, Would, Can, and Could:

For the questions starting with these words, the answers should mostly have these words, and sometimes only mentioning them in the answer is enough.

Let's see some of them. For example:

- Do you believe in God?

  Yes, I do.

- Did you talk to her?

  Yes, I did.

- Will you come tomorrow?

  Yes, I will.

- Would you like to go for movies?

  Yes, I would love to.
  Or
  Yes, I would.

- Could you help me with this question?

  Yes, I could.

- Can you lend me your notebook?

  Yes, I can.

- Did you participate in the annual function?

  Yes, I did.

- Did you know he was coming?

  No, I did not.

- Would you do this to your friend?

No, I would not.

VII
Chapter 7: Weather and Climate

Weather and climate are used interchangeably by many of us. But both are as different as the sun and the moon.

Weather and climate are two such words that are more or less thought of as one. This misconception sometimes leads to misinterpretation of the meaning.

Let's read out loud about them:

Weather is something that changes frequently and is not long term. Every place in this world experiences a different weather every day. Sometimes it is pleasant, and at other times, it's not so favorable. Breezy, windy, pouring, rainy, sunny, chilly, freezing, stormy, etc. are some of the terms that we use frequently to describe the weather conditions of a particular area.

On the other hand, climate means the long-term pattern of the weather of a particular area. In simple words, the weather that prevails for a long term in an area defines the climate of that area.

<u>For example:</u>

The climate of Rajasthan is dry, which means there is not much rainfall in the area of Rajasthan, so it is kind of dry. But the weather in Rajasthan is breezy, which means at some point of time, the weather there is cool and breezy.

- _Let's find out how to ask about the weather and climate and some of the replies:_

1. How is the weather outside? (बाहर कैसा मौसम है?)

- The weather is stormy outside. (बाहर तूफ़ान आ रहा है।)

1. How is the weather today? (आज कैसा मौसम है?)

- It's pouring today. (when it is raining) (आज बारिश हो रही है।)

3. How is the weather at your place? (आपके वह कैसा मौसम है?)

- It's sunny here. (यहाँ धूप निकिली है।)

4. What is the climate of Karnataka? (कर्नाटक राज्य की जलवायु कैसी है?)

- Karnataka has a humid climate. (कर्नाटक जलि की जलवायु में नमी है।)